A souvenir guide

Greenway
Devon

Jo Moore & Simon Akeroyd

National Trust

Foreword

Here Agatha's grandson, Mathew, shares some of his memories of Greenway, the 'paradise' he enjoyed as a boy and in which he still takes great pleasure today.

Greenway has always been a happy house. My first experience of it was in the late 1940s, with my family trying to recover from a war that deprived me of my father in 1944. The US Coastguard occupied Greenway during the war (they loved it too!) and when they left, the family returned. It was Greenway that saw the first green shoots of a recovery in morale among my family. Greenway is like that!

For a small boy it was paradise: plenty of space, in my case to play cricket or tennis; plenty of attention from a small and adoring family; and the river with all the pleasure boats steaming up and down. Now there is only one paddle steamer left, but they were a magnificent sight. We played clock golf on the lawn above the garden and ate peaches from the greenhouse. It was English countryside at its best – not pretentious but satisfying and relaxing.

Apart from a few professional friends coming to stay (immediately examined by me for any cricket or tennis potential) there was very little mention of books or archaeology. Greenway was, is, and I hope always will be, a place for holidays.

Over this contented scene, my grandparents (whom I called Nima and Max) presided with patience and happiness. I would visit Greenway with my mother Rosalind and, after she remarried in 1949, my stepfather Anthony. By the time

we assembled at Greenway in late July, my grandparents had usually spent time in Iraq and Nima had written a book. My parents ran a market garden in our home in Wales, and everybody was ready for a holiday.

When I visit Greenway nowadays, and go around the well-known landmarks – the Library with its wartime frieze, the Drawing Room where Nima sometimes read us one of her stories, the Boathouse, the view down the river from the Top Garden, and the magnificent collection of magnolias and camellias – I have got over the feeling of nostalgia. Rather, I am delighted that, through the National Trust, many more families now have the chance to experience Greenway's magic and to realise that it is, indeed, an important landmark in England's green and pleasant land.

In a society of almost continuous change, Greenway is reassuringly constant, and I hope it does not change too much, and that you all continue to enjoy it as I and my family have been lucky enough to do all my life.

Opposite The archway to Greenway's Camellia Garden

Above Mathew and Agatha at Greenway

The Famous Mrs Christie and Other Stories

'I am many things: good-tempered, exuberant, scatty, forgetful, shy, affectionate, completely lacking in self-confidence, moderately unselfish…'

Such is the manner in which this greatly loved, award-winning author described herself in her 1977 autobiography. Much is written about her extraordinary literary achievements but Greenway, her beloved holiday home, allows us to explore her more personal and relaxed side.

An imaginative and adventurous child, Agatha had a huge zest for life, for which she was always thankful. She was a woman of many passions – people, dogs, houses and their furnishing and decoration, tea parties, music and theatre, trains, swimming in the sea, surfing and drinking cream amongst them. Once saying that the two most exciting things in her life were her car, a Morris Cowley, and dining with the Queen at Buckingham Palace, Agatha was a modest and generous woman, relishing holidays spent with her family and friends, and even finding time to be a governor at the local school in Galmpton.

Agatha at Greenway

Young Agatha

Born in Torquay in 1890, Agatha spent a happy childhood there at the family home, Ashfield. Surrounded by a loving family and looked after by 'Nursie', a very important figure in her early life, she fabricated a world of make-believe around her, creating adventures with her wooden hoop and an imagined group of girlfriends, each with their individual character. Her first dog, a gift on her fifth birthday, inspired a lifelong love and she was rarely without one.

Agatha was educated at home and did not go to school until she was a teenager. Her childhood was one of great variety and many influences, her family living abroad between 1895 and 1896. Formally trained in music and singing at a finishing school in Paris, her ambition to become a professional singer was thwarted by her shyness in public performances; her love of the piano, however, continued throughout her life.

Aged 20 Agatha spent a winter in Egypt with her mother, where she enjoyed the social life – indeed, she has vivid memories of her first evening dress – but was, as a lively young woman, less keen on the antiquities of the country; her interest in these developed later in life. During the First World War Agatha was a nurse in a Red Cross hospital in Torquay town hall and qualified as a pharmacist dispenser. During this time she met Archie Christie. They were married in 1914 and their daughter Rosalind was born in 1919, just after the end of the First World War. They spent nearly a year travelling around the world together in 1922 but the marriage ended in 1928.

Right Agatha served as a nurse with the Red Cross in Torquay

'One of the luckiest things that can happen to you in life is, I think, to have a happy childhood.'

An Autobiography, Agatha Christie, 1977

Above Agatha with surfboard

Below Agatha and Archie Christie

Mrs Mallowan

Following her divorce from Archie, Agatha decided to fulfil one of her long-held dreams and caught the Orient Express to Ur in Iraq, where she was intent on pursuing her interest in archaeology, the seed of which had been sown when she had travelled to Egypt with her mother. There, the following year, she met Max Mallowan, the archaeologist-in-training on the site. After a brief courtship they were married in Edinburgh in 1930. Their marriage lasted for 47 years. Together, in 1934, they bought Winterbrook House in Wallingford, Oxfordshire, which was to remain their main home for the rest of their lives.

Agatha buys her 'dream house'

On one of her visits to Ashfield, in 1938, Agatha saw Greenway advertised for sale in *Country Life* magazine. Agatha and Max went to see the house, which she had known since childhood, and thought it the ideal holiday retreat, especially when Agatha discovered that the sale price was £6,000, not the £16,000 she had initially thought.

In her autobiography, Agatha relates: 'We drove home talking about it. "It's incredibly cheap," I said. "It's got 39 acres. It doesn't look in bad condition either; wants decorating that's all. "Why don't you buy it?" asked Max. I was so startled, this coming from Max, that it took my breath away.'

Agatha had a bit more planned for Greenway than redecorating. Having resolved to buy it, Agatha approached her friend Guilford Bell, an architect she had met on an archaeological expedition to Syria, engaging his services to make Greenway the perfect home from home.

Two months later, the house was hers. Guilford had suggested some changes, including demolishing a wing built in 1892, installing new bathrooms and lightening the dark rooms with cream interiors.

to the Drawing Room and the mahogany doors protected with plywood nailed over their fronts. During the War Agatha moved to London, fearful that she would never see Greenway again, and worked as a dispenser at University College Hospital. Refusing to use the shelter during air raids, she slept in her bed, with her fur and hot water bottle close by. Max joined the Royal Air Force and was sent to the Middle East, the couple's first separation in ten years.

A place of recovery and hope

At the end of the War, in 1945, the Mallowans returned to Greenway. The house had seen a few changes in the intervening years – 14 lavatories had been installed along the service corridor and a frieze had been painted along the walls of the Library. The furniture, however, was undamaged, save for a little carpet moth and a few damp books.

Greenway at last became the perfect family holiday home for which Agatha had so longed. Indeed, the house so inspired her that she used it as a location for two of her best-known books – *Dead Man's Folly* and *Five Little Pigs*.

Left Max and Agatha Mallowan

Below First-edition covers of *Dead Man's Folly* and *Five Little Pigs*

Assisting the war effort

Less than a year later the Second World War was declared and Greenway was requisitioned by the War Department, first for child evacuees and then by the Admiralty for the U.S. Navy. From 1944 to 1945, 50 men from the 10th Flotilla of the U.S. Coastguard occupied Greenway as an officers' mess. An inventory of the contents of the house was made in 1942, the furniture moved

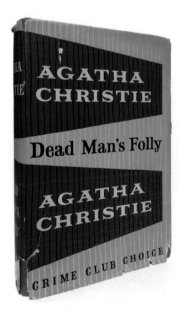

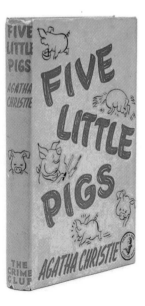

Agatha and the archaeologist

Meeting Agatha on one of his expeditions in Ur, Max had found her 'immediately a most agreeable person'. (Interestingly, in her autobiography, while extolling the virtues of her father, Agatha placed great emphasis on the quality of agreeableness.) On an early trip together to see local places of interest, their car became stuck in sand and a long wait followed whilst help was sought. Rather than becoming agitated, Agatha's response was simply to settle in whatever shade the car afforded and to go to sleep. At this, Max decided that 'she must be a remarkable woman' and would make an excellent wife.

After their marriage Agatha accompanied Max, soon to be one of England's most celebrated archaeologists, on excavations in the Near and Middle East, providing, in addition to her sense of humour, much other support.

Archaeological discoveries

From Ur they moved on to Nineveh, where they discovered the outstanding collection of ivory carvings at Nimrud, 600 of which the British Museum later acquired for £1.7 million. Later they went on to discover the extraordinary potter's shop at Tell Arpachiyah.

Political difficulties in Iraq forced them to move to Syria, where Agatha wrote of their lives on archaeological expeditions in her book *Come Tell Me How You Live*, published under the name A. Christie Mallowan. After a break during the Second World War the Mallowans eagerly returned to the Middle East. Agatha wrote:

'With enormous pleasure we started off once more … to resume our work in the Middle East. No Orient Express this time, alas…. This time we flew.' Their second visit to Nimrud covered 13 sites over a period of ten years and is described in Max's book *Nimrud and its Remains, Volumes I and II* (1966).

Life on expedition
During this time Agatha's knowledge of archaeology grew, along with her love of what the study revealed about how people lived and their craftsmanship. She worked alongside the archaeological team, photographing, drawing,

cleaning (using her face cream!) and mending the finds excavated. Indeed, Max was to praise her with the words: 'Don't you realise that at this moment you know more about pre-historic pottery than almost any woman in England?'

In 1958 Max made his last expedition to Nimrud. Already Professor of Western Asiatic Archaeology at London University, he was honoured as a Commander of the British Empire (CBE) in 1960, matching Agatha's CBE of 1956, and knighted in 1968. Max published the story of his life in his book *Mallowan's Memoirs: Agatha and the archaeologist* in 1977, the year before his death.

Above Max and Agatha poring over archaeological documents at their home in Wallingford

Right Agatha took great interest in her husband's archaeology

Left Max and Agatha on expedition

Enjoying family time

Greenway made the perfect family holiday home and Agatha and Max spent many weeks here each year during the spring and summer, often joined by family and friends. Agatha always came here to celebrate her birthday and Christmas.

Greenway was in its heyday from the 1950s, when it was the centre of the family's recovery from the War. The guest book for the years 1939 to 1976 shows a steady flow of visitors, both large house parties and individuals. The book includes such visitors as Allen Lane (founder of Penguin Books and Agatha's publisher), Edmund Cork (her literary agent) and the Gilbert family of nearby Compton Castle (now owned by the National Trust), whose predecessors had built the original Greenway Court.

Fun and relaxation

The relaxed feel of Greenway was noticed and loved by everyone who visited. The Dining Room was the social hub of the house, with the quieter pursuits of reading and writing taking place in the Drawing Room. Here Agatha would also play the piano but, still suffering from shyness, only when no one was listening. A small staff was employed at Greenway, with a minimum of a butler and housekeeper, and the addition of a cook when the family was there.

Outdoor entertainments also played a big part of life at Greenway. Games such as cricket, tennis, clock golf and croquet were played regularly and, with its proximity to the river, the family would watch boats on the river in the afternoons.

Above Agatha and Max at Greenway

Confessions of a crime writer

'I well remember all our family and friends filling up various confessional albums belonging to my grandmother, great aunt and so on. Everyone enjoyed it immensely.'

Agatha in an interview with Michael Parkinson in 1973

Your Complexion. List low pardoner

Your favourite virtue. Loyalty

Your favourite qualities in man. Courage and Gentleness

Your favourite qualities in woman. Warm hearted + Gay

Your favourite occupation. Sitting in the sun doing nothing

Your chief characteristic. Disturbing interfering

Your idea of happiness. Sunshine - Quietness

Your idea of misery. The people I love to go away — Grey skies

Your favourite colour and flower. Mauve, Lily of the Valley, Magnolia

If not yourself, who would you be? An Opera Singer

Where would you like to live? Devon and in the Orient

Your favourite prose authors. Dickens, Elizabeth Bowen, May Sinclair, Maugham

Your favourite poets. Herrick, Coleridge, Eliot

Your favourite painters and composers. Holbein, Giotto, Corot, Elgar, Bach, Vaughan Williams

Your favourite heroes in real life. Sir Philip Sydney - Test Pilots

Your favourite heroines in real life. Edith Cavell. Amy Johnston

Your favourite heroes in fiction. Rhet Butler (Gone with the Wind)

Your favourite heroines in fiction. Viola in Tasker Jevons

Your favourite food and drink. Fruit - Lobsters - Cream. Roast Beef. Good Water

Your favourite names. Viola, Rosalind, Celia. Richard. Edward.

Your pet aversion. Crowds, noise, Parties, Too much Conversation

What characters in history do you most dislike? Jacob.

What is your present state of mind? Deeply happy

To what fault have you most toleration? Idleness - Lies

Your favourite motto. Speech is Silver, Silence Golden.

April 19 1954

Agatha Mallowan

Above One pastime enjoyed by all generations of the family and also in the company of friends was filling these albums of 'confessions' with thoughts, fancies and favourite things; this page completed by a 'deeply happy' Agatha in the spring of 1954

Making a gift of Greenway

Agatha's only grandchild, Mathew, was born in 1943, from Rosalind's first marriage to Hubert Prichard, and together they lived in Pwllywrach, Hubert's family home in South Wales. After his death in action in France in 1944 Rosalind continued to live 'in the big empty house' in Wales with Mathew. Agatha recalled him as 'an enchanting little boy, and always, in my memory, such a happy little boy'.

Rosalind married Anthony Hicks in 1949. Rosalind, Anthony and Mathew would visit Greenway in the holidays, and all had great affection for the place. When Mathew married in 1967 and took over his father's house in South Wales, Rosalind and Anthony made Devon their permanent home and moved to Ferry Cottage, on the Greenway estate.

A home for Rosalind and Anthony

When Max died in 1978, outliving Agatha by two years, Rosalind and Anthony moved into Greenway House. Anthony's great interest was the garden and he managed the commercial nursery, which had been started in 1949 and continued until the end of the 20th century. Rosalind's skills in managing others were well established from childhood when, as Agatha describes, she was 'the kind of child who likes to be highly organised' and for whom holidays had 'never a moment's leisure for anyone'. These talents were later concentrated on running the family business of Agatha Christie Ltd, which had been set up in 1955 to oversee Agatha's literary estate. Mathew described his mother as 'solid, dependable, enjoyable and very occasionally wilful'.

Far left Agatha and her grandson Mathew

Above Summer days at Greenway

Top right Anthony ran Greenway's commercial nursery for decades

Left Mathew, Rosalind and Anthony taking a stroll about the grounds

Thoughts of the future

The Hickses spent many happy years at Greenway, but their thoughts began to turn to the future of the house. Feeling that the National Trust would be suitable guardians of the estate, and following discussions with its staff, the decision was made by Rosalind and Anthony (and Mathew, who had become a joint owner in 1991) to gift the garden and estate to the charity in 2000. The gardens opened to the public later that year. Rosalind and Anthony continued to live in the house, their privacy protected by the trees surrounding it, until their deaths.

When Anthony died in 2005, a year after his wife, discussions about the house and its collections were held between the National Trust and Mathew. His mother had made it clear in previous discussions that she did not want the house to become a 'Christie theme park' but had confidence in the Trust's approach, confirmed by the sensitive restoration of garden buildings it had already undertaken.

Getting Greenway right

In 2005, after Anthony's death, a full inventory of Greenway House was made, the contents remarkably similar to those listed in the 1942 inventory. Mathew continued to live at Pwllywrach in South Wales, and generously offered a large part of the collection at Greenway to the National Trust. So began a new phase for the house: 'Another Chapter'.

This was the name given to the National Trust's major project that began in 2007 to restore the house and collection and to open it to visitors. For two years and at a cost of over £5 million – £4.5 million of which came from the Trust's own funds plus a grant of £800,000 from the Heritage Lottery Fund – the project involved the emptying of the house of all its contents in order to undertake major structural work to the building, especially vital being the roofs and foundations. This work is now virtually invisible. Alongside this, conservation work was carried out on the entire collection.

Working together

Mathew was hugely supportive of the project and helped the Trust to understand how the family lived there and how the collections had been put together. Discussions with him led to the decision to restore the house to its 1950s heyday, when it was the centre of the family's recovery from the War.

Whilst the building work was going ahead, undertaken by local contractors, the huge task of conserving the contents, which numbered around 20,000 items, began. All but the larger objects, which were put into local storage, were moved into what was fondly called 'The Shed'.

In reality a series of seven linked Portacabins, of which six were storerooms and one a workspace, they were the centre of a hive of activity. Led by the Trust's Regional Conservator, a team of dedicated volunteers cleaned, listed, labelled and photographed each item, an enormous and meticulous task. Under the guidance of a specialist conservator, simple repairs were made to damaged books and items on paper were transferred to conservation-grade materials.

The house was opened to visitors in February 2009, and once again the house, garden and estate are reunited to be enjoyed and discovered by visitors, as Agatha and her family once did.

Far left A volunteer in Greenway's garden

Left A conservator cleaning a Tunbridgeware box

Above Turning the clock back to Greenway's holiday home heyday

Greenway, the Perfect Getaway

'They drove away from the station over the railway bridge…. The road forked and … passed into thick woods … down a steep hill … through big iron gates … along a drive, winding up finally in front of a big white Georgian house looking out over the river.'

Still recognisable from this description in *Dead Man's Folly*, the approach to Greenway by road remains unchanged since Agatha wrote these words in 1956. The Italianate-style lodge marks the start of the estate from the road. Following the drive, laid out in the 1820s in a sweeping style made fashionable by landscape architect Humphrey Repton, the house appears. Set on a wooded hill, high above the River Dart, the site (described by Max as 'a little paradise') was first chosen for a dwelling in Tudor times, when Greenway Court was built for the Gilbert family. The family moved to Compton Castle in around 1700 and Greenway Court was demolished.

Today's house, built in the 1790s, follows the Georgian style in its central block. Materials from the previous house were used in its building and evidence has been found of its courtyard under the present Entrance Hall (see over). The Elton family added the Dining and Drawing Room wings, with their colonnaded porticos, to the central block in 1815. Richard and Susannah Harvey, who owned Greenway from 1852 to 1882, concentrated on the garden and estate. They had the interior of the house redecorated by the firm of Cowtan & Son from Oxford Street in London, whose archives are now in the Victoria and Albert Museum's collection. Later, in 1892, the Bolithos built a new east wing, housing a billiard room and study, with bedrooms above. This wing was demolished in 1938, when Agatha bought Greenway, and the house today is as she left it.

Visitors can also arrive from the River Dart by boat, reaching the Boathouse on the quay (see page 52). From here a zigzag path leads steeply through the garden to Greenway House.

Opposite **Greenway overlooking the River Dart**

Right **Visitors arriving by ferry**

The Entrance Hall

Part of the 1790s house, this room is little changed, with the exception of the under-stairs cupboard, which was fitted by Agatha in 1938. It contains remnants of the flock wallpaper left over from the 1868 redecoration of the house. The original stone-flagged floor from Greenway Court was discovered under the current floor during building works.

Five generations of collectors

The Entrance Hall, through which Agatha, Max and their family and guests would have entered the house, is the same one used by visitors today. It gives a taste of the home you are invited to explore and discover, a home created and developed by the family, which contains the results of a lifetime of collecting, a passion shared by five generations.

Agatha's love of collecting was instilled in her as a child, from her grandparents and parents, when she treasured the penny monkeys she acquired at a local fair. Her passion was passed on to her daughter and grandson and was continued until the family left Greenway. When living at the house, the family loved to go to the local salerooms, to support local artists and craft workers, adding to their ever-growing collection.

Right The entrance to Greenway

Far right Agatha's beloved 'Nursie', by Nathaniel Hughes John Baird (1865–1936)

Family matters

A notable and unusual object in the room is the brass-studded Zanzibar-type chest, or 'kist'. This would have originally been used to hold a woman's dowry, such as linens, on her marriage. An example of such appears in two of Agatha's books, *The Mystery of the Baghdad Chest* and *The Adventure of the Christmas Pudding*. The family stored dressing-up clothes in it. The Hickses clearly enjoyed playing games together, represented here by croquet sets, fishing rods, tennis racquets and golf clubs.

Portraits in the Entrance Hall also evidence the importance of family to Agatha and the Hickses. Of particular interest are the paintings of Agatha's paternal grandparents, her sister Madge, brother Monty and her beloved 'Nursie'.

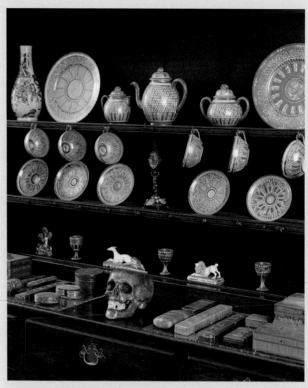

An eclectic collection

Comprising over 12,000 items, the collection covers a huge range of dates, from pre-historic archaeology to modern paperbacks and studio pottery. Some passions were shared by several members of the family, whilst others were an individual interest. The straw work boxes and Tunbridgeware introduce the visitor to the breadth of the family's collecting interests, the boxes having been collected by Agatha. Part of Anthony's large collection of hats can be seen here, piled informally on top of a marble bust. The collection of 40 bottles of homeopathic medicine, contained in a purpose-made wooden box, gives a hint of Agatha's pharmaceutical knowledge and qualifications; more than sufficient to use with authority when poisoning her characters. Also striking a rather sinister note is the distinctive skull-shaped porcelain jar on the dresser. Made in Japan in the late 19th century, Max used it to store his tobacco.

The Morning Room

Originally used as a sitting room, this space was commandeered to house the family's growing collection. There is a great variety to be seen, with some of the items coming from Agatha's childhood home, Ashfield, and others from the Wallingford house.

The room has been little changed since the 1790s, the only additions being the alcoves designed by Rosalind and Anthony in the 1970s to display the collections. The nail marks in the mahogany doors, the first of several seen around the house, are the result of the U.S. Coastguard's attempts to protect the fabric of the house during the Second World War.

Family treasures

Much of the furniture came from Ashfield and was collected by Agatha's parents and grandparents. Rosalind bought the Louis XV-style chair with the flower-moulded frame from the collection of English writer William Makepeace Thackeray.

Many of the ceramics on display in the room were made by the Swansea and Nantgarw factories in Wales. Of particular interest are the items of botanical porcelain, much loved by Rosalind and Anthony.

Displayed in the glass-panelled cabinet, or vitrine, is an eclectic and fascinating array of pocket watches, snuff boxes and miniatures, probably collected by Rosalind.

'One unpleasant winter's day, I was lying in bed recovering from influenza. I was bored. I had read lots of books ... and was now reduced to dealing myself bridge hands. My mother looked in. "Why don't you write a story?" she suggested. "Write a story?" I said, rather startled. "Yes," said mother. "Like Madge". "Oh, I don't think I could." "Why not?" she asked?'

An Autobiography, Agatha Christie, 1977

Left A collection of pocket watches and snuff boxes

Agatha and Rosie

Prominently displayed is the portrait of Agatha Mary Clarissa Miller. Entitled *Lost in Reverie*, it was painted by the American artist Douglas John Connah. It shows Agatha at the age of four, clutching her beloved doll, Rosie.

The very same doll is also on display. Rosie was made in France by the company Jumeau, which was famed for making dolls with beautiful faces and detailed clothing that followed the contemporary fashions. Rosie is made from bisque porcelain, an unglazed ceramic, which was chosen as it gave the doll's skin a realistic appearance.

Left Agatha Mary Clarissa Miller aged 4, *Lost in Reverie*, by Douglas John Connah (1871–1941)

Below Agatha's doll Rosie

This informal and spacious room, added to the Georgian central section in 1815 to mirror the Dining Room on the east side of the house, captures best the spirit of Ashfield, with Agatha's parents' and grandparents' ornaments.

A space much used by the family during the daytime, it was here that they and their close friends relaxed and were entertained. Her grandson Mathew has happy memories of Agatha reading the latest manuscript of her book to friends and family, wanting to test the plot and its plausibility on a live audience. Used to store all the furniture in the house during the Second World War, it is now comfortably furnished with a sofa and armchairs.

With large windows leading onto the garden, the room originally only had one internal door, to the right of the fireplace, with the other door being false for the sake of proportion and symmetry. Leading to the Winter Dining Room, this second door was opened up by the National Trust, in order to allow better visitor flow around the ground floor of the house.

Agatha the musician

The piano in this room, made by Steinway, was frequently used by Agatha. She took it with her to London when Greenway was requisitioned during the Second World War, and there it survived damage during a bombing raid.

Agatha was a talented pianist and, having shown ability from a young age, trained as a concert pianist at finishing school in Paris. She even composed a waltz, when she was just seventeen years old. However, her performance was hindered by shyness in front of an audience, which prevented her from pursuing a professional musical career.

On the piano are displayed family photographs.

Agatha the writer

Agatha would sit at the desk in this room to do her correspondence, read over her scripts and jot down notes for her books.

Other items of particular interest in this room are the *Commedia dell'arte* porcelain figures, which belonged to Agatha's grandmother. They became the inspiration for the characters in her book *The Mysterious Mr Quin*, in which Mr Quin is actually 'Harley Quin'.

Left Agatha at the piano in the Drawing Room

Right This harlequin is one of a set of six *Commedia dell'arte* figures by Samson, Edme et Cie

The Winter Dining Room

This cosy room, used by Rosalind and Anthony as a dining room in the colder months, was used to store much of the large collection of china, glass and other items. The floor-to-ceiling built-in cupboards installed in the 19th century were perfect for this purpose. The room originally had three doors; one, between the cupboards, is now hidden. It would have led directly to the kitchen behind and ensured that food arrived at the table hot – particularly important in the winter.

The plaster overmantel is thought to have been originally part of Greenway Court. Its whereabouts until it resurfaced in 1964 are unclear, but at that time it was bought on behalf of the family for £20 and installed in this room.

On display

The items displayed in the cupboards encompass a wide range of objects collected by family members. Prominent amongst them is the silver – a passion for both Agatha and Max, who had set themselves a goal of collecting a piece from every year from the mid-17th century to the accession of Queen Victoria in 1837. Agatha, as all serious collectors would have done, kept a detailed book of all the purchases she made.

Hiding places

The large Chinese temple, made from lead-glazed stoneware, dates from the early 17th century. An unusual and highly detailed piece, it was used by the family to hide eggs at Easter for egg hunts. It used to stand outside the Drawing Room but was brought inside by the National Trust due to the deterioration it had suffered caused by frost.

Now proudly displayed in this room is Agatha's Dame of the British Empire Award. Typical of her modesty, this was found by the National Trust tucked at the back of a shelf in one of the cupboards, but has now been given the prominence it deserves.

Left This early 17th-century stoneware temple was once a hiding place for Easter eggs

Above This plaster overmantel is thought to have been part of Greenway Court

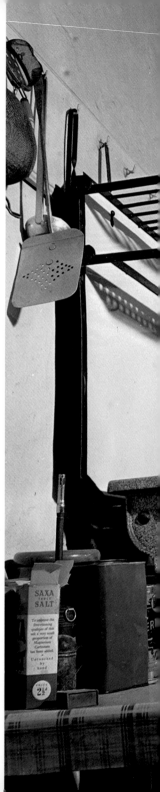

The Kitchen

Although normally the domain of the cook, when the family was staying Agatha used to prepare simple meals here from the recipe books that are still in the room. The kitchen is much as it was, with the fitted dresser mentioned in the 1882 sale particulars still *in situ*. The old range cooker has been replaced by the current Aga, but the hot closet and soot box, marked with the maker's name, are as provided by Jeakes of London in the 19th century.

Rooms for the servants

The Butler's Pantry off the kitchen is part of the 18th-century service wing and is lined with cupboards, some dating from that time and some from the 19th century. The bottles in the pantry are left over from house parties, some even having the signatures of guests.

The Service Corridor links the service wing to the Entrance Hall and was used by the staff. It still retains its original 18th-century stone-flagged floor, under which was discovered the cobbled front courtyard of Greenway Court. Although replaced by Agatha in 1938, the original box of the servants' bell system still remains.

'The best time to plan a book is while you're doing the dishes.'

Left Agatha in her kitchen
(not Greenway)

The Main Stairs

This space has seen a few changes since it was built in the 1790s. In 1832 the Elton family altered the 18th-century staircase and added the Marwood and Elton family arms on the ceiling bosses. The arched window on the half-landing is described in the 1882 sales catalogue. Agatha's only alteration was to replace the coloured glass in this window with clear, in 1938.

Take time to stop and stare

Running up the stairs, the lithographic prints were collected by Agatha's American grandmother. Lithography is a printing process that involves making copies of an artwork using a flat metal surface or stone. These were printed in colour by Nathaniel Currier, after Louis Maurer. Maurer was the last surviving artist known to have been employed by the firm Currier & Ives, which prided itself as being 'The Grand Central Depot for Cheap and Popular Prints'.

Displayed in a niche on the half-landing, the magnificent 4th-century sculpture of a seated Buddha was found by Max on one of his expeditions. He left it to the British Museum in his Will, with the proviso that it remained at Greenway during Anthony's lifetime; particularly fitting given the latter's Buddhist interests. It is now on long-term loan to the National Trust, still mounted on the original plinth made by Anthony.

Up on the main landing, the circular bookcase was commissioned by Rosalind in 1984 from David Charlesworth of Bideford. Designed in the Arts and Crafts style to house the collection of her mother's paperback editions, these are all still in place as they were then.

'The smallest room'

In a small room off the landing is the lavatory, little changed since its installation in the 19th century. The mahogany seat from the lavatory, original to the house, was one of the few luxuries, in addition to a soft down pillow, which Agatha insisted on taking with her on archaeological expeditions with Max.

The Bedroom

This beautifully proportioned room was chosen by Agatha for its stunning views over the garden and river. It was also used by the 10th Flotilla Commander and his two deputies in the Second World War. Hercule Poirot, too, made it his room in *Dead Man's Folly*.

' Little changed since Agatha's time, the room and its furnishings evoke the 1950s and early 1960s. The National Trust's major building project did little to change the room, with even the scratch marks left by Anthony's dog, Cheeki, still visible on the door.

Apparently very comfortable, the campaign bed in this room belonged to Max and was used by him, first on his military campaigns during the War and subsequently on archaeological expeditions. The other bed is not Agatha's but a replacement for the original.

Agatha herself made the needlework fire screen, taught the skill by her grandmother.

Fairytale furniture
Bought by Agatha in Damascus in 1929, the mother-of-pearl inlaid chest was described by

Left Agatha at her typewriter in her bedroom, the Damascene chest behind her

Above Agatha's bedroom with the Damascene chest in the very spot Agatha chose for it

The Dressing Room

This small room, leading off Agatha's bedroom, is fitted with floor-to-ceiling wardrobes along its length. In here are Agatha's and Rosalind's clothes, both everyday and evening wear, as well as dressing-up clothes used by all the family. Suitcases are stacked against the wall, as if in preparation for a voyage abroad.

Agatha remembered packing for expeditions in her book *Come Tell Me How You Live*: 'One thing can safely be said about an archaeological packing. It consists mainly of books... I am firmly convinced that all archaeologists pack in the following manner: ... they fill [their] suitcases to the brim with books. They then, reluctantly, take out a few books, and fill in the space thus obtained with shirt, pyjamas, socks etc.'

her as 'the sort of furniture that reminds one of fairyland'. Clearly a piece much cherished by Agatha, it has occupied pride of place in her bedroom since she brought it to Greenway.

Seemingly made from wood, the papier-mâché furniture in this room was collected by Agatha. She recalls in her autobiography seeing a papier-mâché washing-up bowl being used by a servant girl when she was a child, so this is perhaps where her fascination with this material began.

Right Blue leather travel cases in the Dressing Room

The Fax Room

A small room with beautiful views down the garden to the River Dart, this was used by Max as his dressing room and situated beside his bedroom next door, now the Sitting Room. It is fitted with large wooden drawers and tall cupboards, with a marble-topped section for a washstand. When Anthony and Rosalind moved into Greenway the room became an archive room. Anthony's study is now within the holiday apartment, so the National Trust has furnished this room with his office equipment, including the fax machine that gives the room its name today. The malachite desk set and typewriter also belonged to him.

A complete set of first editions of Agatha's books is on display in the room, as well as the picture of the Sad Dog, upon which she based Bob in *Dumb Witness*. The rare and extensive collection of Stevengraphs was collected by the whole family. These are pictures woven from silk on a Jacquard loom, originally made by Thomas Stevens, a weaver who lived in Coventry in the 19th century. They became popular amongst collectors in the 1960s and 1970s, during the revival of interest in Victorian items.

Right Stevengraphs are pictures woven from silk originally created by Thomas Stevens in the 19th century

The Sitting Room

Originally one of the principal bedrooms of the house, this room was initially used by Max as a bedroom and study, and subsequently became his writing room, where he wrote up his notes from his various expeditions in Tell Brak, Chagar Bazar and Nimrud. It was converted into a sitting room by Rosalind and Anthony, who furnished it with comfortable sofas. The long sideboard was installed by the National Trust, replicating what had been there in the Hickses' time, and here you can find further information about Max's outstanding archaeological career and achievements.

The glazed niches were introduced by Max to display some of his finds. A collection of envelopes in a sideboard drawer, addressed to Agatha, is testimony to her fame – one being simply addressed to 'The Greatest English Detective Writer, Devonshire, England'. Her travels with Max were to inspire the settings for her books *Murder in Mesopotamia* and *Murder on the Nile*.

Much of the collection of studio pottery and contemporary paintings belonged to Rosalind and Anthony, although the portrait of Agatha by Nathaniel Hughes John Baird, painted in 1910 when she was 20 years old, predates these. Baird, known also for his equestrian paintings, was an artist favoured by the family and there are other works by him around the house. The photograph of Slipper, the last cat to live at Greenway, is displayed on a chest.

Left The Sitting Room was previously used by Max as his study

Above First-edition covers of *Murder in Mesopotamia* and *Death on the Nile*

The Library

The Library was the original dining room of the 18th-century house but changed to its current function when the Dining Room wing was added in 1815, the scar visible on the wall marking the old doorway from the Entrance Hall. At this time the room was panelled in teak, but this was removed by Agatha, on Guilford Bell's advice, and he also oversaw the installation of the fireplace, originally in the Inner Hall.

Mathew's favourite room

Acting as a 'mess room' for the U.S. Coastguard in the Second World War, with a bar set up in one of the alcoves, it was later used as a sitting room by the Hickses. The room was Mathew's favourite in the whole house and left the deepest

impression on him as a child, a feeling which remains unchanged by the National Trust's restoration work. The central chandelier, which would have hung here as they would have done elsewhere in the house, was removed by Agatha, as she disliked overhead lights. Instead she replaced them with table and standard lamps, creating more gentle pools of light.

The bagface sofa and three chairs came originally from Ashfield. They are so called because they are covered in 'bagface' Turkish carpet and velvet. The collection of ceramics displayed in the glazed cupboard shows some pieces of studio pottery, by Bernard Leach and Lucie Rie amongst others, collected by Anthony. The Bargeware along the bookcases was from Max's collection, as were the wooden figures, which came from North Africa when he was an Intelligence Officer during the Second World War.

Images of war

The most striking and extraordinary feature of the Library is the frieze that runs along the upper section of most of its walls. Painted in 1943 by Lieutenant Marshall Lee, it charts the 10th Flotilla's journey to Greenway from Key West in Florida at the start of the War. The image of Greenway appears above the door and includes an Infantry Landing Craft in the river below.

Left The 10th Flotilla sets out from Key West

Right Agatha in the Library

Books, books and yet more books

The lower bookcases that line most of the room were installed by Agatha in 1938 and the upper parts added by the Hickses in 1982. They contain most of the 5,000-strong book collection in the house, which gives a good feel for the varied interests of different family members. Ranging in subjects from local history to Buddhism and from gardens to antiques, amongst them is the collection of Greenway Editions of Agatha's books. A book entitled *The Historian as Detective* may give some clue as to why Agatha was so passionate about archaeology, and the room could well have been the inspiration for the setting of her book *The Body in the Library*.

Below First-edition cover
of *The Body in the Library*

The Dining Room

Echoing the Drawing Room on the west side of the house, this room was also added by the Elton family. Of beautiful proportions and lit by large windows on two walls in the daytime, the room was used by the family for more formal dining, when the butler would serve the dishes, and for family gatherings.

Agatha's 60th, 70th and 80th birthday celebrations were held here, on 15 September, with the last being preceded by a picnic on Dartmoor. The grand supper that followed is testimony to Agatha's passion for food and for the pleasure of sharing it with friends and family. The menu began with avocado vinaigrette, followed by homard [lobster] à la crème, with ice cream and blackberries à la Greenway to complete the meal. Although Agatha was teetotal, the meal was accompanied by Krug Champagne ('non-vintage') and water. It's not difficult to imagine the extended family gathered around the large mahogany dining table for this celebratory occasion.

Behind closed doors

The pair of elegant curved mahogany doors at the end of the Dining Room conceal, to the right, the butler's storage cupboard and, to the left, a corridor to the Lobby, which still retains a fragment of wallpaper from the 1860s. Again, as in the Library, the central ceiling light was removed by Agatha, although the delicate ceiling rose remains, and at night the room is lit with lamps.

The table is laid with part of a dinner service of limited edition Royal Worcester ware, decorated with scenes originally painted in watercolour by John James Audubon, the American ornithologist and painter, who became best known for his extraordinary *Birds of America*, which included 435 life-size hand-coloured prints of nearly 500 species of bird.

Below A birthday luncheon

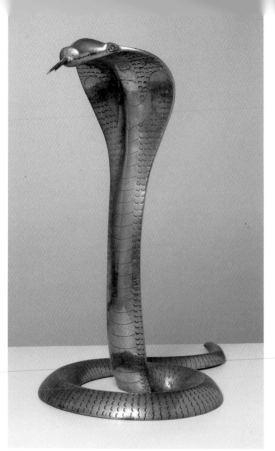

A camel, a lobster and a cobra

The pottery bactrian (two-humped) camel, displayed on a side table, is decorated in a type of glaze called 'Sancai', which was used on Chinese pottery and in mainly three colours: brown, green and an off-white cream. It dates from the Chinese Tang Dynasty (618–906 AD) and was a gift to Agatha from Max. She originally kept it in her bedroom. The two pole screens, to either side of the fireplace, were embroidered in silk by Agatha's grandmother.

A quirky reminder of one of Agatha's favourite foods is a ceramic dish featuring a large lobster. By the door stands a cobra doorstop, its forked tongue protected by a cork ever since Agatha snagged her stocking on it.

Top left The cobra doorstop on which Agatha stuck a cork to save her tights

Above This pottery Bactrian is over a thousand years old and was a gift from Max to Agatha

Left This ceramic dish gives a clue to one of Agatha's favourite foods

The Inner Hall

This room, probably the billiard room described in the 1832 sale details – relocated when the 1892 extension was built – was used by the family most often to enter the house and also as a post room, with letters arriving or awaiting posting being placed on the central table. Decorated in a light cream colour scheme by Guilford Bell, it houses a large 'Constor' heater, installed by the Hickses. Although rather incongruous today, it is an interesting example of 20th-century country house technology.

Against this background is displayed another large and eclectic collection of items gathered by five generations of Agatha's family. The 1942 inventory shows that many objects were in the same places then as now.

A variety of ornaments includes intricate boxes and papier-mâché objects collected by Agatha. Mauchlineware boxes were extremely collectable in the mid-20th century, and naturally made their way into Agatha's collection. Produced from the 1820s to 1933 in an East Ayrshire town after which they are named, these souvenir wooden boxes depict the places they were first bought.

Anthony's hats are piled up on the central table, on top of one of his pieces of studio pottery. Also once belonging to Anthony is the mobile phone, so antiquated by today's standards, which he used when he was working in the garden.

The 17th-century armchair, bought by Agatha's mother Clarissa Miller, comes from Ashfield and the archive still retains her receipt for this purchase, together with a sketch of the chair she included in a letter to her husband. A collection of family photographs is displayed on a chest.

Above **The eclectic collections continue through to the Inner Hall**

Left **These souvenir Mauchlineware boxes were highly collectable**

The Lobby

When the Victorian extension, which included a billiard room and study on the ground floor, was demolished by Guilford Bell, he replaced it with this 'modernist' porch in 1930s taste. Used as a garden entrance by the family, it was a practical space, with plenty of room for wet coats to be hung to dry and its tiled floor being forgiving for muddy boots.

Sparsely furnished with two small tables, the only decoration consists of framed items on the walls, including a portrait of Anthony Hicks by Anthony M. Devas. Devas, who began his studies at the Slade School of Art aged 16, was a well-known portrait painter, elected to the Royal Society of Portrait Painters and also an Associate of the Royal Academy.

Nearby hang a planting plan and list. These show the position of individual plants in the garden, identified by numbers, which cross-reference to the list in the 1980s.

So now we make our way to the garden, through the back door, passing a small and rather battered frog, as Anthony might have done on a fine day, wearing his sun hat and clutching his mobile phone, to admire Greenway's horticultural collection.

Left The way to the garden, passing a portrait of Anthony Hicks by Anthony M. Devas

'The Loveliest Place in the World'

Greenway garden is nestled in a superbly picturesque spot on the banks of the River Dart. On the edge of wildness, it must be one of the most romantic gardens in the country.

Each year spring-flowering shrubs such as magnificent magnolias and raucous rhododendrons jostle for position amongst over 150 varieties of camellia. The gardens have a sense of nostalgic timelessness, with the sound of passing pleasure boats mingling with the whistles of the nearby steam train and the clink-clink coming from the yachts moored below. This is where Agatha Christie came to relax and unwind, taking a break from the hustle and bustle of life as a world-famous author. Now open to the public, everyone can experience what led Agatha to describe it as the 'loveliest place in the world'.

Left The garden at Greenway enjoys an aspect few can match

Above Agatha admiring a magnificent magnolia bloom

The Main Drive

All grand houses deserve an entrance worthy of their status and Greenway is no exception. The majestic, sweeping drive starts at North Lodge, an Italianate-style building constructed in 1850 that bears the crest of the Harvey family, the Cornish chough.

From here the drive curves down under the canopy of 200-year-old beech trees and past rare trees and shrubs lining the driveway. One of the most impressive specimens in spring is the magnificent sweet michelia (*Magnolia doltsopa*), with its large, cream, sweet-scented flowers. There is also a good collection of eucryphias, which are native to South America and eastern Australia but manage to thrive in the mild Greenway climate. In late summer they are clothed in scented white flowers that contrast well with their grey evergreen leaves. The large-leaved oaks are also worth noting, with a Japanese emperor oak (*Quercus dentata*) and Mongolian oak (*Q. mongolica*) on the journey down to the house.

Sheltered by the walls

The bothy borders flank the path that leads towards the Tennis Court and walled gardens. They contain a mix of planting, including sub-tropical style plants enjoying the shelter of the warm walls such as the kahili ginger (*Hedychium gardnerianum*), abutilons and cestrums that jostle for space with a large holly-leaved sweet spire (*Itea ilicifolia*), whose hanging catkin-like flowers in summer are honey scented and frame the entrance to the Tennis Court. Opposite, there is a beautiful tree known as a harlequin glorybower (*Clerodendrum trichotomum*), with impressive bright-blue fruits appearing in late summer.

Below The Main Drive

The Tennis Court

Constructed within one of the smaller walled gardens lying to the north-west of the house, the Tennis Court is surrounded by impressive borders, packed with notable specimen trees and shrubs all thriving in the warm, sheltered conditions.

Probably one of the most significant trees in the garden is the large Campbell's magnolia (*Magnolia campbellii*), planted by Max in 1938. It takes a notoriously long time to produce flowers and Max had to wait around 20 years for this spectacular tree to bloom. He would often write home when on his archaeological travels abroad to check on its progress. The gardeners at Greenway eagerly watch each year to see when this magnificent tree will produce its large, bright-pink flowers, often using it as a bench mark for how warm and mild the winter has been. Usually it flowers in mid to late February but it has been known to flower as early as mid-January.

A horticultural mystery

Alongside the south side of the Tennis Court is another imposing shrub, a rhododendron from the 'smithii' group (*Rhododendron smithii*), with its huge multiple trunks twisting upwards towards the sky. In the wintertime the bare stems can look magical when the rain intensifies its unusual red colouring. One of the horticultural mysteries at Greenway is whether this is a single plant that has sent out branches close to the ground that have taken root, or whether they are lots of individuals. Whatever the answer, it is certainly a dramatic feature.

Specimen trees

The sunny, sheltered borders around the other sides of the Tennis Court contain a further range of specimen shrubs and trees, including the dove tree (*Davidia involucrata*) with its unusual, long white bracts looking like handkerchiefs (it is also known as the handkerchief tree). The tree fuchsia (*Fuchsia excorticata*) is one of the largest types of fuchsias you can grow. The Judas tree (*Cercis siliquastrum*) is unusual for its bright pink flowers borne on bare branches in spring before the leaves appear.

Above The sprawling *Rhododendron smithii* by the Tennis Court

Left The Judas tree (*Cercis siliquastrum*) in flower

The Peach House and North Walled Garden

Dominating what is currently used by National Trust gardeners as a working propagation and nursery area, is a beautiful lean-to peach house. It is certainly the longest peach house in Devon, possibly in the country.

Dating from the mid-19th century, it was restored in 2010 and the peaches, apricots and nectarines inside are grown in the same way as they were when mentioned in *The Garden* magazine in 1901: 'trained on the back wall and over a semi-circular trellis in front of the path'.

In the section at the back of the Peach House are examples of different fig varieties grown as standards in terracotta pots. One of the more curious varieties is 'Panache' with its small, striped green-and-yellow fruits looking like mini hot-air balloons.

A growing business

Established in 1947, the Greenway Nursery ran in the North Walled Garden until the 1980s and was managed by Agatha's son-in-law, Anthony. The surrounding glasshouses are used by the garden team to propagate and 'grow on' plants for the garden, continuing the tradition of plantsmanship that Greenway's various owners were famed for.

The other glasshouses include a historic melon house, a propagation house and a potting shed. Within the Melon House is a small collection of Chilean bellflowers. Cold frames and lining-out beds are dotted about, adding character to this working nursery. Towards the end of the North Walled Garden is a grove of figs, originally planted as standards during the Bolitho period and now left to run rampant, creating a lush thicket of fruiting trees.

Enduring beauty

In her autobiography, Agatha writes about returning to Greenway after the war, poignantly describing it as 'wild, wild as a beautiful jungle. Paths had disappeared, the kitchen garden, where carrots and lettuces had been grown, was a mass of weeds, and the fruit trees had not been pruned. It was sad in many ways to see it this way but its beauty was still there.'

Left The Peach House

The South Walled Garden and Vinery

Here Anthony grew and sold a range of interesting and rare plants, all propagated on site. Today this area features a large central lawn, the ideal spot for relaxing, picnicking and generally whiling away the time.

The outside borders are packed full of rare and often exotic shrubs. Some of the more interesting plants include the thorny anchor plant (*Colletia paradoxa*) at the far end of the southern wall, and a box-leaf azara (*Azara microphylla*), an unremarkable Chilean evergreen shrub for most of the year until its scented flowers arrive in early spring to fill the air with the delicious smell of hot chocolate. Later in spring, an ancient Chinese wisteria (*Wisteria sinensis*) climbs the wall behind the herb border in spectacular cascades of blue.

A fruitful garden

The Vinery was built sometime between 1839 and 1865. It originally housed a fine collection of ornamental plants and was restored by the National Trust in 2005. Today it contains a range of tender and half-hardy plants, but also includes the grapevines after which the building was named.

The South Walled Garden also features vegetable beds with some of the produce used in the café. There are also old apple trees espaliered along the edge of the walled gardens, remnants of a former kitchen garden. At the far end of the South Walled Garden on a raised terrace is an allotment looked after by the school children of Galmpton Primary School, where Agatha Christie was once a governor.

Left Inside the Vinery

The Dahlia Border

Perhaps one of the most significant features of the garden in summer is the Dahlia Border, designed and planted by the great lady herself.

The show-stopping Dahlia Border lies in front of the Putting Green (where Agatha Christie and her family enjoyed the gentle but competitive pastime of Clock Golf, mentioned in *Dead Man's Folly*). Many of Agatha's original planting choices are still thriving, whilst the hellebore border on the other side of the path owes its existence to her daughter Rosalind's passion for these shade-loving plants.

To the west of the Putting Green is an ornamental grass and bamboo border adding all-year round interest.

Dahlia for murder

Agatha's short story, *The Four Suspects*, is a classic tale of murder and suspicion, secret societies and coded messages, in which Miss Marple and a friend solve a deadly puzzle that has defeated Scotland Yard's finest, armed with nothing more than their knowledge of horticulture and a nurseryman's catalogue. The riddle in a random letter is solved when Miss Marple recognises some familiar dahlia cultivar names – 'Dr Helmut Spath', 'Edgar Jackson', 'Amos Perry', 'Tsingtau' and (here's a twist) 'Honesty' – making up the acronym DEATH. When this is combined with an old-fashioned knowledge of the language of flowers (dahlias are synonymous with treachery and betrayal), Miss Marple is quickly able to name the culprit.

The Fernery

Sometimes referred to as the Fountain Garden, the Fernery has a cool and relaxed atmosphere, where its shade provides a stark contrast to the warmth and sunny aspect of the walled gardens.

The design was created by Susannah Harvey, Richard's widow, sometime in the mid-19th century, and consists of a series of narrow paths set amongst slopes of fern-covered rock leading to a circular pond and fountain at its centre. This two-tiered Coalbrookdale piece is made from cast iron and may well have been installed at Greenway before 1839.

Here in the Fernery's melancholic atmosphere, Agatha and the Hicks family chose to bury their dogs throughout the 1970s and 1980s, and the graves can be seen on the south-west ridge.

Variety in the Fernery

Jostling for position among the ferns are the fluffy flower heads of strawberry saxifrage (*Saxifraga stolonifera*). The collection of ferns includes the unmistakeable shuttlecock or ostrich fern (*Matteuccia struthiopteris*) and an impressive collection of basket ferns (*Drynaria* spp).

Separating the Putting Green from the Fernery is a rare, white form of Judas tree (*Cercis siliquastrum*) and a fine dogwood tree (*Cornus kousa*), which produces spectacular coloured foliage and attractive red fruits in winter following an impressive show of large, white flower bracts.

Left An assortment
of blooms from the
Dahlia Border   Right The Fernery

The Hydrangea Walk

Above The Hydrangea Walk

Linking the Fernery with the wider woodland garden and the Top Garden (see page 48) is the more formal Hydrangea Walk, consisting of a box-lined pathway with shrubs such as rhododendrons and hydrangeas planted for seasonal interest on either side. Previously this may have also been the site of a rose walk, which would have included arches for rambling roses to scramble over.

The pathway to the right meanders back down the slope towards the house, which in springtime is carpeted with dwarf narcissi, such as *Narcissus cyclamineus* with its impressive reflexed petals, and delicate cyclamen in among the long grass. Set further back on the grassy bank is the stone sculpture 'Mother and Child' by Bridget McCrumm, gifted to the National Trust by Rosalind.

Towards the bottom of the path is a Chilean wineberry tree (*Aristotelia chilensis*), which in late summer produces 'super fruit' packed full of vitamins, minerals and antioxidants.

At the bottom of the grassy bank is the Coalhouse, once a gardener's bothy, now converted for use as a toilet for visitors. A periwinkle (*Vinca* 'Dartington Star') clothes the steep bank, producing amazing deep-purple, star-shaped flowers from late winter onwards.

Around the house

On the east side of the house is one of the most significant areas of the garden, the Rockery. Constructed using limestone boulders by the great Exeter nursery Veitch & Sons in collaboration with the local landscaper F.W. Meyer, this area once contained a wide variety of alpine plants, some of which remain, alongside numerous species of tulips and narcissi planted by Rosalind. Beautiful acers still grow in amongst the rocks. A black mulberry (*Morus nigra*) grows out of the grass bank to the side of the Rockery and is laden with raspberry-like fruit in late summer.

Memorable views

At the front of the house the expanse of formal lawn slopes gently down towards the river. Dotted with snowdrops in late winter and followed by snake's head fritillaries (*Fritillaria meleagris*) in spring, this area is the perfect place to relax and admire similar views to those Agatha would have enjoyed. There are some spectacular magnolias planted near the house, including

Anthony's favourite to the east, 'Kew's Surprise', with vivid bright pink flowers. Probably the most notable is the *Magnolia veitchii*, planted by Max in the centre of the viewpoint to celebrate the end of the War.

Striking plants

On the west side of the house is the croquet lawn with a mixed border as a backdrop, planted up with a range of herbaceous perennials, including sub-tropical plants such as the tall Chinese rice-paper plant (*Tetrapanax papyrifer*) and the giant viper's bugloss, or tower of jewels (*Echium pininana*). If you look carefully, you will also discover an air-raid shelter hidden among the plants towards the back of the border.

Both ends of the house are dominated by imposing evergreen specimens of large-flowered magnolia (*Magnolia grandiflora* 'Exmouth'), planted in 1893 and which produce large, white flowers with a gorgeous lemony-vanilla scent from mid to late summer.

Above *Magnolia campbellii* 'Kew's Surprise' in flower in spring

Left *Magnolia grandiflora* 'Exmouth'

The Top Garden

Basking in the warmth of the Devonshire sun (when it makes an appearance) is the Top Garden, sometimes referred to as the Hot Border, which enjoys additional shelter from the wall that runs along the back of the bed. The border itself is packed full of flamboyant and exuberant plants such as the Californian poppy (*Romneya coulteri*), agapanthus, crinums and red hot pokers, all blooming profusely throughout the summer months in this heat trap.

At the end of the border is a structure that was originally a summerhouse but was used more recently as a tool shed. The outlook at the end of the border is one of the finest in the country, with stunning views over the River Dart towards Kingswear and Dartmouth.

Rare and individual

The slope below contains the last remnants of the nursery based here during Anthony's time. Today, the grass area is packed full with exotic-looking plantings such as phormiums and puyas. Their incongruity amongst the old apple trees is a useful reminder that Greenway is a place of surprises. To add to the Top Garden's individuality, a glossy, evergreen escallonia (*Escallonia illinita*) scents the whole area with curry.

Behind the Top Garden and running parallel with the south lodge drive is the Plantation, which contains many rare trees and shrubs. The main path back towards the house has many more impressive specimen trees to admire, including the foxglove tree (*Paulownia tomentosa*) and another handkerchief tree.

The Bird Pond, The Far End Path

Towards the end of the upper middle path is the quarry that provided the rock for the surrounding landscape. The area is now home to a Bridget McCrumm sculpture of a bird, hence the name. The pond itself was once bigger but appears to have been filled in with rubble, possibly from the alterations made by the Mallowans in 1938. It has recently been cleared and replanted to display the quarried cliff and the sculpture to better advantage. Now water lilies adorn the surface of the pond, while Siberian irises (*Iris sibirica*) provide additional interest around the edges. Plantings of shrubs such as acacia soften the edges of the harsher stone landscape, while bamboo provides screening, giving an intimate feel to the area.

Determinedly growing
Around the corner from the Bird Pond heading up the hill are some huge tree ferns (*Dicksonia antarctica*), some upright, others surviving the destructive impact of past storms and growing almost horizontally. There is also a large clump of black bamboo (*Phyllostachys nigra*) and an impressive evergreen magnolia (*Magnolia delavayi*) that was planted around 1880. It too fell over in a storm and had to be cut back, but has recovered well in the years since.

Down the garden path
The Far End Path leads up to the warmest and sunniest part of the garden, but winds its way initially through a shady walkway. Most notable are the two huge griselinias half way up the path, a plant normally reserved for hedging in seaside towns, which have been allowed to flourish naturally and become fully mature trees. If you look carefully on one of them you can see a huge aerial tree root growing out of the trunk about halfway up, looking like a horse's tail.

Left **Red hot pokers in the border in the Top Garden**

Right **The Bird Pond**

The Primrose Bank

The middle path from the house runs parallel with the river and passes banks decorated with primroses and bluebells in spring. Imposing Japanese cedars (*Cryptomeria japonica*) dominate the start of the middle path with their mighty boughs and textural trunks, creating a suitably shady atmosphere as one moves away from the house and into the woodland garden.

A clump of 'Blue Wave' hydrangeas appropriately cascades down the bank towards the foot of the zigzag track. The banks on either side are scattered with impressive specimen trees such as the sweet gum (*Liquidambar styraciflua*) with its amazing, reptilian-like branches and foliage that release a scent to match its name when torn.

Dotted around are a Persian ironwood tree (*Parrotia persica*), the wood of which is so dense it doesn't float, a dogwood (*Cornus controversa*), with tiers that cause some to know it as the wedding cake tree, and a beautiful birch (*Betula jacquemontii*), its pure white trunk creating a stark contrast to the darkness of the River Dart below.

An eastern feel
Taking the lower fork of the central path eventually ends up at the Kwan Yin Pond. There is a distinctly Oriental feel to this area

Above The River Dart glimpsed through the specimen trees scattered over the banks

Right The Kwan Yin Pond, named after the statue in the centre by Nicholas Dimbleby

with a stunning Japanese maple (*Acer palmatum*) providing purple and crimson foliage in autumn. Clumps of bamboo give an intimate feel to this part of the garden.

The central feature is the Kwan Yin sculpture, created by Nicholas Dimbleby and framed by a beautiful camellia, 'Cornish Snow', with its pure white flowers.

On the opposite side of the path from Kwan Yin is a series of ponds following the slope downwards. Towards the bottom of the path is a sunken circular structure, which is thought to have been an icehouse.

The Boathouse

The Boathouse, known locally as 'Raleigh's Boathouse', was so called because Sir Walter Raleigh, half-brother to Sir John Gilbert who built the original Greenway Court, was a frequent visitor to the house. The original structure on the site was built around the 16th century, when a provisions store would have stood on the quay, giving trade links to Dartmouth and Kingswear downstream and to Totnes upstream. The river's depth, 50 feet in mid-channel, made it ideal for the anchorage of larger vessels.

The first mention of a boathouse was in the late 1700s but the present two-storey building dates from late Georgian or early Victorian times, a rare survival of a boathouse with a plunge pool. Repair of damage caused during the Second World War was paid for by the Admiralty, who anchored the landing craft of the 10th Flotilla off the Boathouse, ready for training exercises. The plunge pool, mentioned in 1839 records, is at river level and would have been used for 'taking the waters', salt-water bathing being thought to have medicinal benefits. Above the plunge pool is the saloon, an airy room with a balcony, two fireplaces and a few pieces of cane furniture, perfect for bathers who had just used the plunge pool. It was here, above the river, that Agatha gave parties and hosted barbecues. Mathew, who moored his boat *The Hope of Greenway* off the boathouse, recalls the place as a 'young person's paradise'. Members of the family would watch boats going up and down the river and look for wildlife along the muddy, tree-lined and rocky shore. Visitors today can experience the same pleasures, with common sights being birds

of prey, waders and occasional kingfishers and voles. There is even a resident seal. A night-time visit could be rewarded with bats hunting along the shore, looking for insects, before returning to their roosts in the Boathouse's rafters.

This special part of Greenway was the inspiration for the location in two of Agatha's books – Dittisham across the river featured in *Five Little Pigs* and a boathouse was the scene of the crime in *Dead Man's Folly*.

Above The Boathouse

Right Agatha and Max by the Boathouse

The Battery

This was another favourite part of the garden, from which Agatha and her family watched passing boats and wildlife. Reached from the main house by a steeply sloping path, the Battery stands high above the river, overlooking it and with views of Dittisham on the opposite side. It is another inspiring location which Agatha used for the scene of a murder, this time in her book *Five Little Pigs*, which she wrote in 1942. In it she described the Battery as 'an artificially cleared plateau with battlements set with cannon. It gave one the impression of overhanging the sea. There were trees above it and behind it, but on the sea side there was nothing but the dazzling blue water below.' The canons are still there, facing out towards the river between the battlements.

An estate map of 1839 shows this structure in its present form and it's thought that the Battery dates from the late 18th or early 19th century. It was perhaps part of the Dart estuary defences during the times of the Napoleonic wars between the French Empire and other European powers. Today, however, the scene is one of utmost peace and tranquillity.

Top right Agatha and Max on the Battery

Right The Battery

The Camellia Garden

Our garden tour culminates with camellias, appropriately, as Greenway is famous for them. The Camellia Garden is a stone walled enclosure, probably originally built before 1832. The remains of a glasshouse can be seen, as when these plants became fashionable in Victorian England, they were considered to require extra protection. However, it quickly became apparent that most camellias are more than happy growing outdoors in the mild Devon climate.

The mature specimens that line the paths may well be originals, left *in situ* when the glasshouse was dismantled. All that remains are the brick flues in the wall, although the aviary built into the wall is still largely intact. There is also a wooden arbour set into the wall with an attractive cobbled floor – an ideal spot from which to watch the world go by.

Other notable plants within the Camellia Garden are the cork oak (*Quercus suber*), referred to in *Dead Man's Folly*, and the impressive Chilean hazel tree (*Gevuina avellana*), with wonderful foliage and edible fruit.

Surprises to the very end

The path through the archway leads to the River Walk, passing a huge sweet chestnut (*Castanea sativa*), possibly the oldest tree on the estate at between 250 and 300 years old. Along the path, remnants of walls and terraces can be seen, built by Spanish prisoners of war taken from the captured warship *Nuestra Señora del Rosario* and put into the keeping of John Gilbert during the failed invasion by the Spanish Armada.

So, right to the end, Greenway and its garden provide dramatic discoveries and intriguing glimpses. Like an Agatha Christie mystery, there are many layers to delve into, secrets to uncover and surprises along the way. You can follow the twists and turns through the garden, then spend an enjoyable time unravelling your way back home.

Above A spectacular specimen in the Camellia Garden

The estate

If you have longer to linger and explore Greenway's wider environs, there are many enjoyable walks, with some wonderful river views. From the car park you can walk to Galmpton and join the Dart Valley and John Musgrave Trails.

The Greenway estate consists of approximately 96 hectares (237 acres), all of which are part of the tenanted Lower Greenway Farm. It includes a Grade II listed parkland and over eight hectares (20 acres) of woodland. The farm itself is a mix of pasture and arable land, with the majority of the enterprise being beef production, although in Agatha's time it was predominately a dairy farm.

Today, the farmland and surrounding hedgerows are managed to attract and provide a habitat for farmland birds such as yellow hammers, linnets, skylarks and the nationally rare cirl bunting, found only in south Devon and Cornwall.

Views to die for

The rolling landscape of the estate has spectacular views over the River Dart. It is crisscrossed with a network of permissive paths and bridleways, allowing visitors to enjoy the beauty of the countryside surrounding the house and gardens. The Dart Valley Trail also runs through the estate linking Kingswear with Totnes.

To enjoy one of the best views of the surrounding countryside, start at the visitor car park and head straight up the hill towards the highest point. In one direction you can see the River Dart flowing down from the rugged Dartmoor landscape. In the other, looking down the river, are spectacular views towards Kingswear and Dartmouth. Directly across the river is the picturesque village of Dittisham, which operates a ferry for visitors to Greenway Quay.

Below Looking over the River Dart towards Kingswear

At the water's edge

Below the parkland on the banks of the river is a large breeding ground for herons, or heronry, the biggest on the River Dart. The best time to view the herons is between March and May from Maple Field, near South Lodge. Here you can see these huge birds landing and launching themselves off the tops of the tall, swaying trees along the banks of the river.

Along the shores of the River Dart, below Lower Greenway Farm, are the remains of an old lime kiln. There are numerous lime kilns in this area of south Devon and they were used to heat up locally quarried limestone, reducing it down to a powder which would have been used for fertilising fields and for the manufacture of lime mortar.

The end of the line

One of the most notable features of the landscape is the railway line that runs through the estate, diving into a tunnel once it reaches Greenway Halt. The railway line was designed by Isambard Kingdom Brunel and the original plan was for it to go all the way to Dartmouth on the other side of the river from Kingswear. However, the railway line was never finished due to financial constraints and the problem of creating a bridge that could straddle the mighty River Dart while allowing shipping boats to pass through. Hence why a railway station was built in Dartmouth but no trains run there. Visitors to Dartmouth instead have to take one of the scenic ferryboat crossings from Kingswear.

Wheresoever and howsoever you travel from Greenway, the staff and volunteers here hope you've experienced and enjoyed some of its unique atmosphere. It's a place redolent with happy family holidays of the past, but helping to make more memories every day.

Right A bird's-eye view of the Kingswear peninsula by George Spencer Hoffman (1875–1950); the railway line is seen running under a tunnel by Greenway and terminating at Kingswear